THE
PRINCIPLES
OF OUR WORLD ™

A collection of stories about how the
PRINCIPLE OF HONESTY
can help us along the journey of life

Written by
David Esposito

HONESTY

Independently published by Harvest Time Partners, Inc.
www.harvesttimepartners.com

Layout and illustrations by Imbue, The Marketing Agency at Digital Dog Direct.
www.imbuecreative.com

For additional information and permissions, please contact:
Harvest Time Partners, Inc.
Attention: David Anthony Esposito
Email: david@harvesttimepartners.com
Phone: 1-877-786-4278 or 269-370-9275

Harvest Time Partners, Inc.
ISBN-13: 978-0692213919 (Custom Universal)
ISBN-10: 0692213910

Dedicated to my Mom and Dad,
Mabel and Anthony Esposito.

Thank you for giving me the gift of a
strong foundation. It has meant more
than you will ever know.

About the Author

David Esposito is a combat veteran, business executive, husband, father, and creator of character-building resources that help individuals, families, and organizations reach their full potential.

He has developed award-winning resources under the brand Character Creates Opportunity®, a character-development initiative designed for all ages. He is also the inventor of Abundant Harvest® and Face to Face®: award-winning conversation games that are being utilized in families, schools, counseling programs, and faith-based organizations worldwide. The games help families and educators open the door to more effective communication and encourage decision making based on principles such as honesty, loyalty, and commitment with the intent of reinforcing the law of the harvest, simply, you "reap what you sow." Abundant Harvest and Face to Face help foster effective conversations on real-world issues and develop the critical life skill of face-to-face communication that is rapidly being replaced by today's online chatter.

David's character and leadership skills were cultivated at West Point and through leadership assignments in the US Army Infantry. As an airborne ranger infantry officer, David led a rifle platoon with the 101st Airborne Division through several combat operations in the Gulf War. He was recognized with a Bronze Star for combat operations in February 1991.

After launching his business career as a top sales representative, David quickly rose through the ranks of corporate America advancing to become the president of a $100-million-plus medical diagnostics company.

David and his wife Tracy founded and sponsor the Harvest Time Partners Foundation, a charitable organization that supports children and young adults in the pursuit of character-building opportunities worldwide. The Foundation supports a wide range of initiatives from college scholarships to community-service projects, as well as international efforts to reduce the suffering of children and young adults.

David provides support to individuals, families, and organizations on a variety of topics and subjects encompassing personal and executive development, team building, leadership training, and building a strong marriage and family. You can contact him at david@harvesttimepartners.com or by calling (877) 786-4278.

Visit www.harvesttimepartners.com to learn more.

What's Inside?

A Note to Parents and Teachers 7

A Note to Children: The Roller Coaster of Life 9

The Principle of Honesty 11

Honesty in Our Home 13

Honesty in Our School 19

Honesty in Our Parents 25

Honesty in Our Work 31

Where Do We Go from Here? 37

Additional Resources 39

A Note to Parents and Teachers in the Home, the School, and the Community

There is no greater impact that we can make in this world than guiding children to develop the skills and abilities to most effectively handle life's ups and downs. Children are the builders of the future for our families and society, and we need to give them the best tools possible.

As much as we would like to "protect" children from the challenges of this world, the reality is that we cannot protect them forever. We would be wise to focus our efforts on preparation rather than protection in order to prepare them for the unavoidable reality that they will encounter challenges during their journey through life.

Aristotle wrote, "Good habits formed at youth make all the difference."

We have a responsibility as parents and teachers to help children form good habits and give them one of the greatest gifts: a strong foundation for living. A foundation that will support them in effectively dealing with the situations they will encounter in life.

There will always be new ideas and new techniques to support us in our changing world. However, even as techniques may change, we need consistent reminders that principles like honesty, loyalty, and commitment will remain the most effective foundation to form our decisions and actions, regardless of the changes in the world around us.

Our hope is that this book will be a helpful reminder to you and the children in your care about the importance of **The Principles** of honesty, teamwork, compassion, courage, and so many others.

The Principles can act as a compass to guide us through all the situations we encounter in life.

The Principles help individuals build and strengthen their character and *Character Creates Opportunity*® for a successful life, regardless of our situation.

*There is a moment of time between our situation and how we respond.
In that moment of time, we have complete freedom to choose our response.
The **inner voice** that drives our response is our **character.***

*The Principles arrive in that moment of time to help guide our response
based on a principle like honesty, compassion, and loyalty,
which will build and strengthen our **character**.*

The Principles bring truth and lend strength to our inner voice.

*As you use this book to help build a strong foundation in children, we hope it also serves
as a good reminder to you about the importance of living a life according to principles.*

A Note to Children

Life is an exciting journey filled with fun, excitement, wonder, and, sometimes, struggles and challenges.

Have you ever ridden a roller coaster?

Life is like riding a roller coaster.

There is so much excitement in the beginning as you get ready to jump in the seat and start the ride. We all must buckle up for safety as the roller coaster will have many ups and downs, twists and turns; so buckling up is the smart thing to do.

There will be times when you will be so high on the roller coaster that you can see everything that is all around you. You will see the exciting turns ahead, and you will know exactly what is coming next.

Then, all of a sudden, you will be in a dark tunnel and a little bit scared because you cannot see what is in front of you.

Then, you speed out of the tunnel into the light again. You're back to enjoying the twists and turns and ups and downs once again.

Life is like a roller coaster ride. This book was written to help prepare you for the "roller coaster" of life.

In this book, you will learn about **The Principles**.

The Principles will help keep you safe during the ups and downs and twists and turns of life, just like the seat belt on the roller coaster.

The Principles will always be at your side to help you during the greatest roller coaster ride—your LIFE!

Now, get ready to buckle up with **The Principles.** Have fun!

The Principle of Honesty

"Hello, I am The Principle of Honesty.

"People say that I am the reminder they need to remain truthful in all that they say and do.

"There will be times in your life when you may feel it is difficult to be honest and tell the truth. You may be afraid of getting into trouble, or you may be worried about what others may think of you when you tell the truth.

"My parents told me that honesty is the best policy, and that is why they named me Honesty.

"Please call on me when you need the strength to be Honest. I can help remind you about how important it is to tell the truth.

"I will be there to support and encourage you— no matter what situations you experience in life.

"Please, count on me to help you be Honest."

Honesty in Our Home

Jenny and her younger sister Elizabeth always enjoyed playing with all different kinds of toys. They had so much fun running, jumping, and playing around. Occasionally, they would have so much fun playing that they would make a complete mess of the playroom.

On one particular day, Jenny became very thirsty and went to the kitchen to get a glass of milk.

She brought the full glass of milk back to the playroom, so they could continue to play.

Jenny and Elizabeth were having fun throwing a ball back and forth.

Jenny tossed the ball to Elizabeth, and it bounced off her hands knocking over the glass of milk.

With a loud thump, the glass fell on the floor; and the milk spilled all over the place.

They stopped suddenly as they heard their mother come into the room.

Their mother screeched and looked at Jenny and said, "Jenny, what happened?"

Jenny was scared because she knew they were going to get into trouble about having milk in the playroom and spilling the milk all over the carpet.

In a moment of time, a number of thoughts raced through Jenny's mind.

Jenny thought: "I could say Elizabeth dropped the ball and caused the milk to spill. I threw the ball perfectly, and she dropped it and caused the mess.

"Maybe I won't get in too much trouble if I tell mom it was Elizabeth's fault."

In that moment of time, The Principle of Honesty came to Jenny's side.

What should I do?

Hi, Jenny. It looks like you might need my help.

"Everyone gets a little scared in a situation like this—especially when you don't know what may happen when you give an honest answer to your mom's question," said The Principle of Honesty. "I know it seems like you may have an easy way out by blaming the spilled milk on your sister, Elizabeth.

"However, as The Principle of Honesty, I want to tell you that you know the truth about what happened. You and Elizabeth were both playing with the ball; and it could have been you, just as much as it was Elizabeth who knocked over the milk. Elizabeth just happened to drop the ball. Remember, it was you who brought the milk into the room in the first place.

"The right thing to do is to tell the truth to your mother."

Jenny, I will be right by your side as you decide what to do.

THE
PRINCIPLES
CHARACTER CREATES OPPORTUNITY
HONESTY

In that moment of time, Jenny thought about what The Principle of Honesty said about being truthful; and she decided what to do.

Jenny answered her mother by saying, "Mom, I brought the glass of milk into the playroom when I knew I should not have done that. I am sorry. Elizabeth and I were playing with the ball. We were tossing it back and forth having a lot of fun. The ball bounced off Elizabeth's hands and knocked over the glass of milk. We should not have been throwing the ball around inside with a glass of milk next to us. I am sorry, Mom."

Jenny's mom was upset with what happened, but she was pleased with the honesty in Jenny's response.

Jenny and Elizabeth were told to clean up the mess quickly and were not allowed to have drinks in the playroom again.

The Principle of Honesty helped remind Jenny about how important it is to always tell the truth.

Later that evening, as Jenny lay in bed ready to go to sleep, The Principle of Honesty came to her bedside.

The Principle of Honesty said, "Jenny, I am really glad that you chose to tell the truth when your mom asked, 'what happened?'

"I know you were scared, but you did the right thing by telling the truth.

"Please remember that honesty is the best policy when you encounter similar situations in life."

Jenny, you can sleep well tonight because you did the right thing today.

Honesty in Our School

Billy is in the fifth grade. On one particular day, he had a very difficult test in math. Billy studied hard to prepare for the test. The entire class was nervous about taking the test because they knew it was going to be a challenge.

The teacher handed out the tests, and the students began to work.

After a few minutes, the teacher announced that she needed to step outside the classroom for a moment and speak with another teacher. She reminded the students to remain focused on taking the test and not to share their answers when she left the classroom.

Just as soon as the teacher closed the door, Billy heard several students talking about the test and discussing the answers to some of the difficult questions. Sally,

who was sitting next to Billy, leaned over and asked, "Billy, what answer did you get for question #5? It is a really tough question; and if I do not get it right, I know I am going to fail this test. Can you help me with the answer, Billy?"

In a moment of time, a number of thoughts raced through Billy's mind.

Billy thought to himself, "I know the answer to question #5; and I really want to help Sally because she is such a nice friend. However, I remember that the teacher told us to stay focused on taking the test while she was gone and certainly not share answers to the test."

"Everyone struggles with wanting to help a friend, even when they know it will break the rules," said The Principle of Honesty. "Sally is really a nice friend, and I know it seems like it should be a good thing to do to help a friend.

"However, as The Principle of Honesty, I want to tell you that you know you would be breaking the rules if you gave Sally the answer to question #5.

"When she left the room, your teacher trusted that you would obey the rules. I know you are seeing everyone else share their answers, but that does not make it right for you to also do the same.

"As difficult as this decision is, I think you know that the right thing to do is to be honest and not share your answer with Sally."

Billy, I will be right by your side as you decide what to do.

THE
PRINCIPLES
HONESTY

In that moment of time, Billy thought about what The Principle of Honesty said about obeying the rules, no matter how difficult it may seem.

Billy answered Sally by saying, "Sally, I really do want to help you; but Mrs. Jones trusted us to obey the rules when she left us alone. She said that we should not share our answers. If I shared my answers that would mean both of us broke the rules. I am sorry Sally, but I am not going to share my answers with you."

Sally was upset, but she understood that Billy did not want to get them both in trouble for breaking the rules.

Billy and Sally went back to working on their tests, and Mrs. Jones soon returned to the classroom.

The Principle of Honesty helped remind Billy about how important it is to be honest and obey the rules.

Later that evening, as Billy lay in bed ready to go to sleep, The Principle of Honesty came to his bedside.

The Principle of Honesty said, "Billy, I am really glad that you chose to be honest and not break the rules when Sally asked you for the answer to question #5.

"I know you really think she is a nice friend, but you did the right thing by saying no.

"Please remember that honesty is the best policy when you encounter similar situations in life."

Honesty in Our Parents

Jessica and her brothers were excited to be on a trip to see their Grandma and Grandpa for the holidays. They had a long drive ahead of them. Sitting in a car seat for several hours was never easy, but they were happy to be on the way to their grandparents' house.

After a few hours on the road, everyone was getting hungry. They decided to go to their favorite fast-food restaurant. However, their dad did not want to waste time in the restaurant and decided to just use the drive-through window; so they could quickly get back on the highway.

They paid for their food, picked up their bag of hamburgers, and were ready to start the drive. Just before they began to travel once again, their father counted the change he received from the cashier after paying for their lunch. He realized that the cashier made a mistake and gave him back an extra $10 bill.

"Hey, look," their father shouted, "the cashier just gave us an extra $10!"

"Yea!" said Brian, the youngest child. "Now, we can buy more candy at the next stop."

"Jim," said their mother to their father, "that nice cashier is probably going to get in a lot of trouble for making that mistake."

Their father replied, "Well, it is only $10, and we have a long drive ahead of us. It will take a lot of time to get waited on once again."

The children sat quietly in the back seat wondering what was going to happen next.

In a moment of time, a number of thoughts raced through Jim's mind.

Jim thought, "I know the $10 does not belong to me. However, it is not my fault that the cashier made a mistake. We have such a long drive ahead of us and it is only $10!"

In that moment of time, The Principle of Honesty came to their father's side.

What should I do?

Hi, Jim. It looks like you might need my help.

"Everyone struggles with money and time, especially on long car trips," said The Principle of Honesty. "I know the kids are tired of driving, and I know you and your wife are tired as well. I also know it may seem that $10 really is not that big of a deal.

"However, as The Principle of Honesty, I want to tell you that you know that the $10 does not belong to you. The cashier was trying to move as fast as she could to get the customers through the line quickly, and she just made a mistake. She will have to pay the $10 back to the store owner at the end of her day when she realizes she is missing $10 in the cash register.

"As difficult as this decision is, I think you know that the right thing to do is to be honest and return to the restaurant to give the cashier back her $10. I am sure it will set a great example for your kids to do the right thing when they find themselves in a similar situation."

Jim, I will be right by your side as you decide what to do.

In that moment of time, Jim thought about what The Principle of Honesty said about not keeping something that did not belong to him—no matter how big or small the amount may seem, he should always be honest when dealing with money.

Jim turned around and said, "Kids, I know we are all tired of driving and it will add more time to our trip; but the right thing to do will be to return to the drive-through and give the cashier her $10."

Their mother turned and smiled at their father and said, "Jim, thanks for doing the right thing."

The Principle of Honesty helped remind Jim about how important it is to be honest, especially when dealing with money.

Later that evening, when they arrived at their grandparents' house, Jessica and her brothers were settling down for bed. Jessica heard someone talking to her father as he rested in bed.

Jessica's father Jim sat quietly in the bedroom when The Principle of Honesty came to his side.

The Principle of Honesty said, "Jim, I am really glad that you chose to be Honest and return the $10 to the cashier.

"I know, at the time, it did not seem like that big of a deal. You did the right thing, even with something as small as $10. That makes me feel good that if you are honest in small things, you will be honest in really big things. It was a great gift to your children to see their dad being honest today.

"Please remember that honesty is the best policy when you encounter similar situations in the future."

Jim, you can sleep well tonight because you did the right thing today.

Honesty in Our Work

Bobby's mother Vickie works in a really big office building. She works really hard and does a great job at work.

Vickie is part of a big team working hard on an important project for the company. One day, the manager of the company saw that everyone was working hard and decided to buy the team lunch.

There were big trays of food because there were so many people working on the project.

Vickie and her coworkers were very hungry because they had been working hard all day without a break.

There was a sign at the lunch counter that said "Please take only one sandwich per person."

One of Vickie's coworkers said, "Forget about that sign, I am taking at least two sandwiches because I am starving. There is plenty of food for everyone to take more than just one."

She turned and looked at Vickie and said, "We are all taking two sandwiches, are you?"

In a moment of time, a number of thoughts raced through Vickie's mind.

Vickie thought to herself, "I know the sign says to just take one sandwich per person because we have a big group to feed. However, there seems to be enough sandwiches that it probably would not make a difference if a few of us took an extra one. Also, I think some of my coworkers might be angry with me if I do not follow along with what they are doing."

In that moment of time, The Principle of Honesty came to Vickie's side.

What should I do?

Hi, Vickie. It looks like you might need my help.

"Everyone struggles with feeling pressure to follow along and do what their friends and coworkers may be doing," said The Principle of Honesty. "In the lunch line, I know it seems like there are plenty of sandwiches for everyone. I know you have been working very hard and are very hungry.

"However, as The Principle of Honesty, I want to tell you that you know there is only supposed to be one sandwich per person. The manager was very nice to buy everyone lunch, and I am sure she knew how many sandwiches to buy for the team. Taking more than one sandwich will not only go against the lunch rule, it may mean that someone at the end of the line may not get a sandwich because there will be none left.

"As difficult as this decision is, I think you know that the right thing to do is to be honest and take only one sandwich."

In that moment of time, Vickie thought about what The Principle of Honesty said about obeying the rules even when it seems like no one else is doing so.

Vickie answered her coworker by saying, "I am only going to take one sandwich for now. If there are any leftovers at the end of lunch, I will see if I can get another sandwich then."

Vickie and her coworkers had a nice lunch and break from their busy project.

Not long after, their boss entered the lunchroom and said that there were several sandwiches remaining; and people should feel free to grab a second sandwich if they wanted another. Vickie decided to grab another sandwich for an afternoon snack, as she knew she had a lot of work ahead of her for the rest of the day.

The Principle of Honesty helped remind Vickie about how important it is to be honest and obey the rules.

Later that evening, Vickie came home from a long day at work. She was very tired; and as she got ready to go to sleep, The Principle of Honesty came to her bedside.

The Principle of Honesty said, "Vickie, I am really glad that you chose to be honest and not break the rules about taking only one sandwich.

"I know it may seem like a small decision, but it was important that you chose to do the right thing and obey the rules.

"Please remember that honesty is the best policy when you encounter similar situations in the future."

Vickie, you can sleep well tonight because you did the right thing today.

Where Do We Go from Here?

"Hello, again. It is me, The Principle of Honesty.

"I hope you enjoyed reading about the different situations in life, and how I can help you to be honest in responding to some pretty difficult situations.

"I want to encourage you to keep working on being honest every day of your life. Just like practicing your favorite sport or playing your favorite instrument, practicing to be honest every day will help you grow stronger in your ability to be honest.

"As you get older, the situations in life will get harder; and you will need to be strong to make sure you can still be honest when life gets more difficult.

"On the next page of this book, there are some situations where you can practice being honest to help prepare you for when you encounter these situations in your life.

"Please call on me when you need the strength to be Honest.

"I will be there to support and encourage you— no matter what situations you experience in life.

"Please, count on me to help you be honest."

What Would **YOU** Do?

We will all experience some situations in life when we should choose to remember The Principle of Honesty.

Below are some sample situations to think about how you would respond.

Remember **The Principle of Honesty**

"What would YOU do?"

You found a wallet with $200 in it on the school playground. There were no pieces of identification in the wallet. What would YOU do?	You are fishing with your friends, and you catch a fish that is two inches smaller than the legal limit to keep the fish. Your friend says, "It is okay, no one will catch you." What would YOU do?
After buying some candy at the store, you realize the store clerk gave you an extra $10 bill when giving you change. What would YOU do?	You were home alone when you spilled a glass of milk on the couch. You cleaned it up as best as you could. When your mom came home, she asked, "Did everything go okay?" What would YOU do?
Your father has been traveling a great deal for work. You wish he would spend more time at home. What would YOU do?	Your parents want to volunteer to be the "parent chaperones" for the school field trip to the zoo. What would YOU do?

Some Additional Resources to Help
Award-Winning Conversation Games

As our world has become more connected with things like the internet, smart phones, and social media, today's online chatter has actually caused our families to become more disconnected; and we are losing the critical life-skill of effective face to face communication.

Harvest Time Partners created a series of conversation games called Abundant Harvest® and Face to Face® to help families and educators open the door to more effective communication and encourage decision making based on principles such as honesty and loyalty with the intent of reinforcing the Law of the Harvest, simply, "you reap what you sow." Abundant Harvest and Face to Face conversation games provide parents and teachers with teachable moments and quality time with their children.

Spend quality time discussing real-world situations with your children and students!

Having a difficult time getting teenagers to "open-up" about dealing with their reality? Abundant Harvest for Teens & Adults can help!

Start great conversations with Face to Face, a fast paced, travel ready conversation game!

Kids Edition

For ages 7 and up

Teen Edition

For teenagers 13 and up

Dinner Party Edition

For ages 18 and up, adults and parents

Visit www.harvesttimepartners.com to learn more!

Some Additional Resources to Help
The Principles of Our World Children's Books

The Principle of Honesty

"People say that I am the reminder they need to remain truthful in all that they say and do."

The Principle of Teamwork

"People say that I am the reminder they need to work together to accomplish great things."

The Principle of Sacrifice

"People say that I am the reminder they need to think about others instead of themselves."

The Principle of Courage

"People say that I am the reminder they need to be brave when they feel worried and afraid."

The Principle of Compassion

"People say that I am the reminder they need to reach out to help people in need."

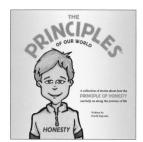 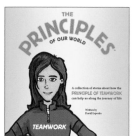 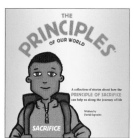 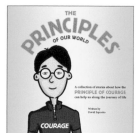 

Visit www.harvesttimepartners.com to learn more!

Made in the USA
Charleston, SC
02 November 2014